Peppertree Press

Catalog 2008

Volume One

the Peppertree Press
Sarasota, Florida

Cover art by Al Mahan, asmahan21@comcast.net

Back cover art by Dillon Koehn, www.dillonkoehn.com

Graphic design by Rebecca Warrick Barbier
beckoecko@aol.com

For information regarding permission,
call 941-922-2662 or contact us at our website:
www.peppertreepublishing.com or write to:

the Peppertree Press, LLC.
Attention: Publisher
1269 First Street, Suite 7
Sarasota, Florida 34236

ISBN: 978-0-9818683-6-3

Library of Congress Number: 2008931336

Printed in the U.S.A.

Printed June, 2008

Welcome

............to the Peppertree Press
Where Seeds are Planted and Flourish Worldwide!

Julie Ann Howell
Publisher/Founder
Email: peppetreepublishing@yahoo.com

Teri Lynn Franco
Editorial Director
Email: tfranco@peppertreepublishing.com

How To Order:

Ingram Distribution: 800.937.8000

Baker & Taylor: 800.775.1800

Books in Print: 888.269.5372

All of our books are returnable.

the Peppertree Press, LLC.
1269 First Street, Suite 7
Sarasota, Florida 34236

941.922.2662

www.peppertreepublishing.com

Fiction

THE ENIGMA

Mike Wall

ISBN: 978-1-934246-61-0

$14.95

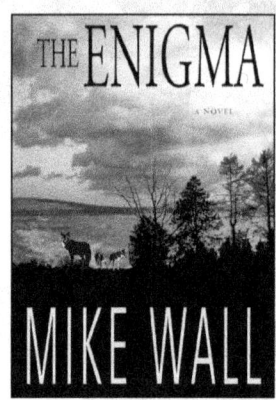

Matt is a typical teenage boy in rural Michigan. While on his annual family hunting trip he encounters a strange, almost mystical pack of coyotes that he cannot seem to escape. The Enigma follows Matt's dilemma to save his girlfriend Ellie from a force more powerful than either of them can comprehend. Matt and Ellie are only teenagers but feel they would do anything for one another. It is easy for one to say they would put themselves on the line for another person, but when the time comes and the beasts have them backed into a corner, how far are they willing to go? Does love conquer all? Love has driven men to war, driven men mad, and has made ordinary men do extraordinary things. The Enigma is a story about the power of love.

KING

Ron Knight

ISBN: 978-1-934246-89-4

$14.95

Explore the world of kings, queens, and lords, along with the people who would die to protect them. Learn about a man who had been cursed with dragon blood flowing through his veins. Thieves, pirates, and assassins divide to aid both good and evil. Peasants are being attacked by outlaws and cities are being robbed by a gang called the Vandals. Over the course of fifty years, six men and one woman discover the difficulties of having the most powerful title in the land...KING.

Peppertree Press ✖

EYE OF THE STORM

James A. Forrest

ISBN: 978-1-934246-50-4

$12.95

In the Eye of the Storm, charter Captain Jack Foster tries to live a simple life and leave his past as a cold case investigator behind him, but when he finds the body of his friend Capt. Tom in the mangroves it's not that easy. When Capt. Tom's killers learn of Jack's interest in the investigation they decide to take care of him and his daughter, Katelyn, before they are discovered. While defending against attack, trying to figure out clues, and protecting his daughter, massive Hurricane Lynn churns in the Gulf of Mexico and is bearing down on them. Out numbered and out gunned, will Jack be able to solve the murder and evade the wrath of Mother Nature or are his and Katelyn's fates sealed like Capt. Tom's?

THE YOUNG GENIUS, A NOVEL OF ENLIGHTENMENT

Dorian Wells

ISBN: 978-1-934246-09-2

Hardcover

$35.95

Rachael Noles, a painter and a poet, is both happily married to a man she loves and content with the life she has. Or is she? One day, a young student named Cabot comes into her life. A painter and a poet himself, Cabot is immediately charming and fascinates Rachael. Wanting so badly to turn Cabot into a successful artist, Rachel is shocked that Cabot is getting in with the wrong crowd. Their intense relationship becomes an obsession for her, as she tries to understand this gifted, yet strange young man. The Young Genius is a poignant exploration of one woman's quest to make sense of an ever-changing world and her place in it.

Fiction

Two Girls Dreams Come True

Kristin Bidzilya

ISBN: 978-1-934246-87-0

$9.95

Two Girls Dreams Come True is about a teenager whose wildest dream came true. Jessica and her best friend Amber travel to the other side of the country on the trip of a lifetime. Jessica and Amber become real stars when Orlando Bloom treats them like royalty. Along the way surprise guests arrive; and Jessica encounters many challenges. Who says all life is perfect? Can Jessica and Amber survive the rush of the life of the rich and famous?

Winter's Last Rose

Denise Elms

ISBN: 978-1-934246-31-3

$19.95

An imperfect life left Rose on the run from a haunting past. Unable to accept the tarnished image of herself, she flees under a new identity to the small town of Briar Glen where she finds an engaging grin, and strong arms. Squire Brodie McBride is a handful in himself. A past including gin parlors and seedier involvements are now eclipsed by God's good word. A man with a determined disposition, Brodie tries to learn what secrets this new stranger in town hides from, while trying to earn her trust before she flees once again. On the run from many demons, not in the biblical sense, Rose slowly learns to enjoy her charming host and his equally engaging family and friends. However a blossoming affection is tempered by a wicked soul that wants to destroy her. All will be revealed, but only if our imperfect Rose understands she is perfect in God's eyes.

Peppertree Press ✣

THE DISCIPLE

Gary Flaherty

ISBN: 978-1-934246-66-5

$14.95

Tucked away in the Appalachian Mountains with its picturesque backgrounds and slow pace of life is the sleepy little town of Pine Valley where every one knows every one... or thought they did. Anthony Stevens a successful business executive, has gone through life as his own God. His wife and only child are ripped away from him and his job is given to someone else. He is about to find out how real God is. While the rest of the town has to deal with unexplained murders and the appearance of demonic beings brought there by the satanic rituals of a cultist group Anthony, Pastor David Berger and County Sheriff Ted Mahoney have the difficult task of bringing these powers of hell to their knees. This fast pace high action story has enough twists and turns to keep the reader wanting more. A disciple has been chosen.

LEARNING TO BE ME

Dr. Karen Hutchins Pirnot

ISBN: 978-1-934246-93-1

$12.95

Peter Michael Henderson is a bench warmer in the Midget Baseball League who has visions of homeruns and accolades for his multivariate and fantasized sports prowess. Instead, in a single moment in time, Peter's life is drastically altered by injury; and he must learn a new way of interacting with his world. Peter is well fortified toward his recovery goal in the tiny frame of Alicia Henderson, Peter's diminutive sister who assumes a "no holds barred" approach to Peter's recovery and reentrance into a world significantly altered by physical incapacitation.

Fiction

THE GOLDEN HARPY II: FEATHER LOST ON THE WIND

S. C. Klaus

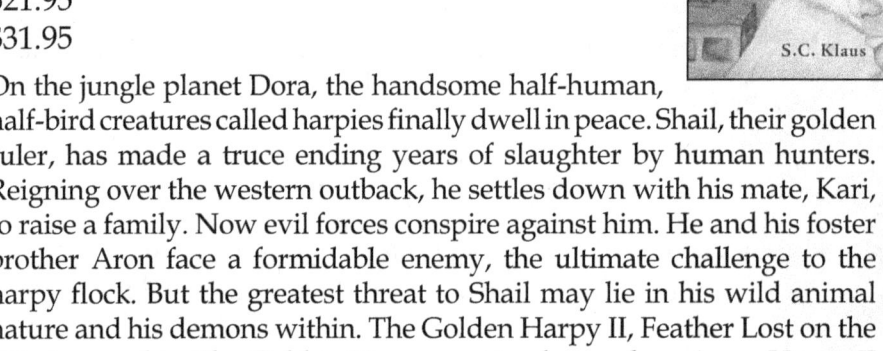

ISBN Paperback: 978-1-934246-19-1
ISBN Hardcover: 978-1-934246-46-7
$21.95
$31.95

On the jungle planet Dora, the handsome half-human, half-bird creatures called harpies finally dwell in peace. Shail, their golden ruler, has made a truce ending years of slaughter by human hunters. Reigning over the western outback, he settles down with his mate, Kari, to raise a family. Now evil forces conspire against him. He and his foster brother Aron face a formidable enemy, the ultimate challenge to the harpy flock. But the greatest threat to Shail may lie in his wild animal nature and his demons within. The Golden Harpy II, Feather Lost on the Wind, sequel to The Golden Harpy, received superb reviews. Harpy II is a fast-paced, action-packed fantasy. It raises a haunting and realistic question: Can the harpies- can nature-survive mankind?

FELINE FOUR

Paul Gerhardt

ISBN: 0-9778525-3-9
$12.95

Feline Four is a collection of four vignettes covering a short period in the life of a Sarasota, Florida family. Seen through the warped mind of author Paul Gerhardt, we follow them on a wacky trip through a series of basic, everyday family problems: drugs, terrorism, bombs, jewel theft, insurance fraud, and neighbors from hell. Hanging tough through it all are Marcie and her worshipful knight in shining armor, Tommy. Feline Four is a light-hearted romp that's sure to entertain.

Peppertree Press

STERLING SLIP

Brink Hudlee

ISBN: 978-1-934246-58-0

$16.00

This is the story of Stuart Sterling who grows up in a small Missouri River community characterized by Scottish high moral standards and clan customs. After moving his family to St. Louis, he starts a climb to first financial success and then political achievement, culminating in the Republican nomination for President when he receives the support of the beautiful Texas Governor Rose O'Daniel. On his way up the business ladder, he "slips" unethical practices into his company's activities. Further "slips" in politics help him position himself to win the national election. Feelings of guilt drive Stuart to an alarming course of action two days before the election. The nation and most of the world are dumbfounded by his attempt at redemption. Sterling's Slip is the first of the Sterling Saga trilogy.

MEET DELANEY

Jackie Mahaney

ISBN: 978-1-934246-63-4

$14.95

The author gives an entertaining peek into the life of a single woman. It is the story of an intelligent young woman who is suddenly dumped by her then "love of her life" husband. From the rebound guy to online dating, we follow her as she navigates through all the twists and turns of being a single woman today.

Fiction

THE LONG WAY HOME

Carol Taylor

ISBN: 978-1-934246-18-4

$17.95

At age 13, Katya is sold to the Gypsy's by her father. Finding the strength to overcome years of loneliness and hardship, Katya makes a brave escape from both the Gypsy's and the oppression of a world war that has affected her native Austria. Leaving friends and family behind she finds sanctuary in a new land to begin life again. Years later, Katya's granddaughter longs to know the her grandmother's story only to discover that there is no such thing as an ordinary life. Experience a journey rich with adversity, fear, courage and love towards The Long Way Home.

THE GATHERERS

Mike Wall

ISBN: 0-9778525-8-X

$14.95

The Gatherers is a psychological thriller in which John, an average everyday family man is attacked by a mysterious intruder with evil intentions. John becomes obsessed with finding out who or what this stranger is. Was it just a burglar? Was it the angel of death? Or was it a Gatherer? Soon the mysterious being starts appearing not only to John but begins to haunt his son, Nathan. The need to protect his family drives John's obsession to the edge of madness building to a final, explosive confrontation that will change everyone's lives...forever!

THE UNREQUITED

Page Brown

Hardcover
ISBN: 978-1-934246-71-9
$34.95

The Unrequited is an incredible story of the turbulent years of the Indochina War seen through the multiple eyes of fictional French and Vietnamese. They live the historical times at the end of the Second World War through the decisive battle of Dien Bien Phu. In this time of revolutionary change French colonials and legionaries are pitted against the followers of Ho Chi Minh and General Giap. Nguyen van Phan, a reporter in exile, leads his new family from a rural village back to Ha Noi to report on the Vietnamese struggle for independence. His wife Thi reluctantly follows. Lieutenant Pasteur, a newly commissioned French Legionnaire seeking adventure, is posted to Ha Noi as a platoon leader. An aging Doctor Ashtray abandons all hope of returning to France and cares for the few remaining French civilians and the growing number of military casualties. The orphan Lao survives in the streets until he is forcibly recruited by the Viet Minh. These lives and others are interwoven in the threads of history, their viewpoints colored by the past and the sights and sounds of the place and era that lead them on separate parallel journeys. Through the years of conflict, they remain unrequited. Not for the faint of heart, this novel portrays the grim face of war. History proved the period just the first act of a much longer tragedy that might have been avoided if America had learned the lesson of those years.

Fiction

Poor Tuggerisms

Jolie Bell

ISBN: 0977852547
$14.95

Have you ever looked at your dog and thought "What on earth is going through that little head of yours?" Wouldn't it be fun to put yourself in your dog's place and think canineishly! Tugger can help you realize this fantasy. He's ready to share some of his deepest (and shallowest) thoughts with you. Join him now for a seriously silly adventure and an inside look at the wacky world of woofers.

he be a rodRent

Barbara Redzisz Hammerstein, a.k.a. Basia

ISBN: 978-1-934246-92-4
$7.95

Barbara Redzisz Hammerstein, a.k.a. Basia, as a small child and a transplant from her beloved Poland, had always yearned to recreate a beautiful and bountiful garden. While singing on the Broadway stage she bought a piece of land in Rockland County in the lower Hudson Valley and began her journey into horticultural and culinary independence. Then an unforeseen battle began as she encountered an elusive enemy that decimated her tender newly planted crops that she with great determination replanted every weekend. One of her new neighbors declared, after listening to her sad tale of woe, that he knew who the stealthy culprit was who had been decimating her vegetables. "he be a rodRent," he advised her and offered to shoot it. She declined the offer and set out to safely rid herself of her elusive adversary. This is her story of that very determined and ultimately successful effort.

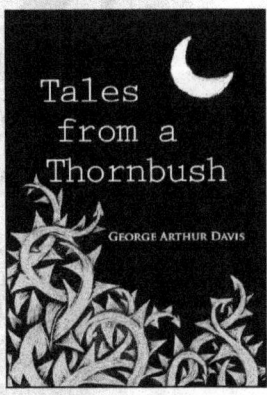

TALES FROM A THORNBUSH

George Arthur Davis

ISBN: 978-1-934246-57-3

$9.95

You will enjoy all of the short stories of anti-heroes in this book, Tales from a Thornbush.

STREET LIFE,
ADVENTURES IN THE ASPHALT CEMENT JUNGLE

George Arthur Davis

ISBN: 978-0-9814894-0-7

$9.95

You will enjoy more short stories of urban anti-heroes at their best from writer George Arthur Davis.

TWO IF BY SEA

Jennifer L. Grant

ISBN: 978-0-9818683-0-1

$12.95

Treasure hunter Zane Alexander is close to finding the mother lode. Searching for the remains of the treasure of the infamous female pirate Anne Bonny, the clues have led him to the Florida Keys, and just when he's close to digging up the truth the past falls in on him.

Non Fiction 2

Write From Your Heart,
A Collection of Memories from Pepper Tree's Past

Compiled by: Julie Ann Howell

ISBN: 978-1-934246-55-9

$14.95

An opportunity is clearly defined as a favorable or advantageous circumstance, or simply a chance of progress or advancement. As the late Eleanor Roosevelt so eloquently stated, "If you prepare yourself...you will be able to grasp opportunity for a broader experience when it appears." A wise woman indeed, if I say so myself, she virtually pinpointed my thoughts when I planted The Pepper Tree Magazine, A Not-For-Profit Literary Venue in the garden of my surrounding communities. For the past three years, talented writers and illustrators of all ages have been submitting to this fine venue to not only receive that byline that they so deserve, but to express themselves with words and art. My Mission Statement: To Give Unknown Writers and Illustrators a chance to become known. As a fund raiser for this magazine and to celebrate their fine work, I have compiled a collection of short stories and poetry entitled, Write From Your Heart. My advice to writers that submit to The Pepper Tree Magazine is to, "Write what you know and write it from your heart." The perfect title for this book… Enjoy!

REPRISE

Rich Brooks

ISBN: 978-1-934246-88-7
$14.95

The dictionary defines reprise as a "repetition of a song or part of a song...To take again." And that's what this book is. A reprise of the columns I've written since, 1997, roughly two years after I was diagnosed with ALS, or Lou Gehrig's disease. I started writing the columns as a way to continue contributing to the daily newspaper, a business that I've been affiliated with since carrying the Citizen-Journal as a boy growing up in Columbus, Ohio. More than words though, these columns are a chronicle of a life with ALS. There's the column I wrote in 1997, lamenting the things I can no longer do. I also tackle some controversial topics, such as potty training, visits from relatives and cutting the lawn. In another way, the columns also chronicle my encounters with technology designed to help me write. In the ten years I've written this column I've gone from typing, to using a voice recognition software to dictating it to a health aid. I now use a laptop computer equipped with text to voice software that speaks for me. It also has in infrared switch that allows me to write. Not surprisingly, many columns deal with family life and struggling to adapt to a degenerative and often terminal disease. What does a war correspondent write about? About the topic that consumes him and is part of his being. I also write about the topics that consume me. Think of me as a correspondent writing from the front of life.

Boomers and Beyond, Prescription for the Golden Years

Heidemarie Rowe, RN

ISBN: 978-1-934246-82-5
$16.95

Boomers and Beyond, Prescription for the Golden Years provides helpful nuts and bolts information for 77 million Baby Boomers and 36 million American Seniors. Fear of declining physical and mental health, losses of loved-ones, financial losses, loneliness and feelings of helplessness when faced with one's own mortality are among those giants waiting to attack. Is there hope and purpose, or is senior life an expected downhill spiral? Seasoned with humor, quotes, lists, personal stories, the author shows how faith, love, and a positive mindset are vital for living the "Golden Years."

The Gift of Knowing, A Journey to Wholeness

Debbie Crews

ISBN: 978-1-934246-76-4
$11.95

The beginning starts with the moment I faced my worst fear which was the death of my child. As long as I live, I don't believe I will ever forget the feelings of shock waves going through my body and the grief that took me to the floor. In that moment, I had no idea that I would ever find a way out of the anguish. However, shortly after, I began a discovery of a deep "knowing" that came from within and guided me through my healing process. It is my deepest desire to share with others, my experience, strength and hope.

IN GOD WE TRUST

Iris Romeo

ISBN: 978-1-934246-99-3

$9.95

Our daughter, Ann Marie, died on November 12, 1990, as a result of a traffic accident while returning home from a college seminar. Her passing has forever changed the lives of everyone who knew her. We all look at things differently now and do not take things for granted. Her memory will always be a part of us all. It is because of her passing and memory that this book came to be. We miss her so much, but know she is still with us and will forever be our angel in heaven.

THE RECEIVER

Joan Howard

ISBN: 978-1-934246-23-8

$14.95

This book is about a little boy who came into the world with a very special gift, an awesome knowledge of the Universe and the desire to help mankind. At the age of two he began telling us about spirits from the other side, about God, the angels, reincarnation, and that the greatest of these is love. He Is the "Receiver."

The Wonder Ears
(or Why Your Kid Won't Go To Harvard)
Facilitator's Manual

Dr. Kelly M. Snell

ISBN: 978-1-934246-54-2

$175.00

Evidence-based, child-centered The Wonder Ears (TWE TM), or, Why Your Kid Won't Go To Harvard parent education curriculum Facilitator's Manual was designed for the audiologist, speech - language pathologist, and/or early intervention specialist. Written in easy-to-understand terms, this curriculum is packed with the facts about chronic otitis media with mild to moderate conductive hearing loss during the insidious disease. In view of the important information research has made available to us in this regard, the fact that inadequate auditory input causes deleterious effects cannot and should not be minimized. This curriculum, a PowerPoint based presentation designed to be used with The Wonder Ears, or, Why Your Kid Won't Go To Harvard participant workbook and The Wonder Ears Parent Education CD, offers the professional a forum for community outreach. This program will empower parents with knowledge in order that they may be informed participants in their child's medical and educational decisions. Both the PowerPoint presentation and the CD are available as online downloads. Please see the Table of Contents page in the Facilitator's Manual for download information. For more information, go to drkmsnell.com.

Peppertree Press ✾

THE WONDER EARS
(OR WHY YOUR KID WON'T GO TO HARVARD)
PARENT EDUCATIONAL
CURRICULUM WORKBOOK

Dr. Kelly M. Snell

ISBN: 978-1-934246-53-5

$30.00

The health care industry must meet the challenge of balancing the cost of doing business with the greater cost of inadequate counseling. The Wonder Ears or, Why Your Kid Won't Go To Harvard participant workbook was designed to be used in conjunction with the Facilitator's Manual and The Wonder Ears Parent Education CD. The PowerPoint-based curriculum was designed for both the extrinsic and intrinsic adult learner. In addition, the facilitator will find suggested uses for TWE TM Parent Education CD throughout the program. The use of the suggested video and audio examples is designed to enhance the visual/auditory encoding of the participants. For more information, go to drkmsnell.com.

CAMPANIA REGION
AN ITALIAN FOOD LEGACY

Anthony Iannacone

ISBN: 978-1-934246-69-6

$26.95

This book hands down many recipes that the Iannacone family has enjoyed for 75 years. The authors parents were from the Campania Region of Italy and the recipes in this book reflect that heritage. Between the pages you will find a variety of Italian recipes from all of the regions in Italy.

Growing Through Grief,
An Adult's Navigation through the Loss of a Loved One

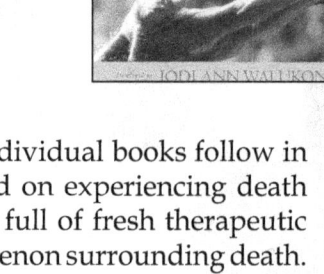

Jodi Ann Walukonis

ISBN: 978-1-934246-37-5

$14.95

Tackling the enigmatic issue of death, three individual books follow in identical outline with age-specific text focused on experiencing death loss as a Child, Teen or Adult. The books are full of fresh therapeutic perspectives as well as basics about the phenomenon surrounding death. A tolerant, spiritual and gentle author's voice facilitates smooth reading of a brutal subject. Grief work and resolving loss in life is beneficial at the personal and universal level and these books cover both.

Griping About Grief,
A Teen's Navigation through the Loss of a Loved One

Jodi Ann Walukonis

ISBN: 978-1-934246-36-8

14.95

Tackling the enigmatic issue of death, three individual books follow an identical outline with age-specific text focused on experiencing death loss as a Child, Teen or Adult. The books are full of fresh therapeutic perspectives as well as basics about the phenomenon surrounding death. The tolerant, spiritual and gentle author's voice facilitates smooth reading of a brutal subject. Grief work and resolving loss in life is beneficial at the personal and universal level and these books cover both.

Peppertree Press ✖

GRAPPLING WITH GRIEF,
A CHILD'S NAVIGATION THROUGH THE LOSS OF A LOVED ONE

Jodi Ann Walukonis
ISBN: 978-1-934246-35-1
$14.95

Tackling the enigmatic issue of death, three individual books follow an identical outline with age-specific text focused on experiencing death loss as a Child, Teen or Adult. The books are full of fresh therapeutic perspectives as well as basics about the phenomenon surrounding death. A tolerant spiritual and gentle author's voice facilitates smooth reading of a brutal subject. Grief work in resolving loss in life is beneficial at the personal and universal level and these books cover both.

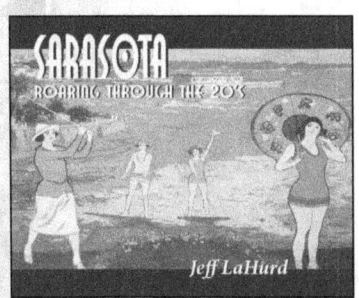

SARASOTA
ROARING THROUGH THE TWENTIES

Only Available from the Publisher   Jeff LaHurd
ISBN: 978-1-934246-20-7

$24.95

Jeff LaHurd's latest book is a look at Sarasota during the Roaring Twenties, when the community came into its own as stripe: snowbirds, speculators, builders and developers, folks looking to make money in the real estate boom, and "binder boy" salesman promising great wealth for those willing to take a flyer on a piece of property. As the rest of the nation, it was an effervescent time here when morals were changing personalities were larger than life, and everything seemed possible. As real estate agent Roger Flory remembered those frenetic years, "There were stacks of checks by every cash register, smiles on every face, money in every pocket...People bought everything they could find to buy."

SOCRATES ONCE SAID

Robert Forman

ISBN: 978-1-934246-68-9

$14.95

Socrates Once Said is a light-hearted look at a serious subject; Alumni relations in support of higher education in America. Inside you will find a complete design on how to initiate and implement an Alumni Association on a university level.

THE MISSING LINK, REVEALING SPIRITUAL GENETICS

by: Richard Gene Arno, PH.D.
and Phyllis Jean Arno, PH.D.

ISBN: 978-0-9814894-2-1

$18.95

This book teaches accountability for each individual's actions and helps the reader understand who God created him or her to be. Our primary goal for providing this book is to help you understand the mysteries of God's wonderful creation of the human race. It teaches how His wonderful plan, for us as individuals, works and how it can cause every person to be happy and fulfilled during this life. It will aid you in developing and maintaining relationships with others, especially with the Lord Jesus Christ.

Peppertree Press ⚇

Unmanaged Care - Ills Of The American Healthcare System

Ken Schields
ISBN: 978-0-9787740-7-3
$16.95

Our American health care system is in need of major surgery. Unmanaged Care takes a look at an ominous side of an industry and a system that is unable - and unwilling - to heal itself. All Americans must be concerned with what's wrong with the system and the issues that continue to drain our finances and take advantage of emotionally-charged health care decisions. Realistic changes can be made. Health care costs can be decreased. We can all become better medical consumers and make a significant difference. Follow the crusade at www.unmanagedcare.com.

Bogies at 12 O'Clock

As told by: Dr. Lucy B. Cole
Author: Jack K. Cole

ISBN: 978-1-934246-13-9
$9.95

Bogies at Twelve O'Clock is a true World War II story that encompasses fascinating and unknown details in the daily life of a prisoner of war in Stalag Luft III in Sagan, Poland. It all started with a surprise early morning wakeup call in Foggia Italy April 23, 1944 at which time Air Corps Bombardier Lt. Jack Cole was ordered to fly with a new crew over the skies to Wiener Neustadt, Austria. This mission turned into an awful air combat fight at which time the back of his B-17 Bomber was shot off. After parachuting out and landing in a newly plowed Austrian field, he was captured and began his 13 months of grueling confinement as a Prisoner of War of the Nazis.

Memoirs

BATTERED HEART

Aina Segal

ISBN: 978-1-934246-06-1

$14.95

In her memoir Battered Heart, Latvian-born Aina Segal, for years a nomadic refugee, now a successful psychotherapist in Sarasota, takes her place on the other side of the couch. Segal, outwardly elegant and self-assured, unzips her heart, spilling out and examining her life as a displaced person. In a world where the media presents horrifying, often mind- numbing news of tragedy, Segal personalizes the cruelty of war and celebrates the strength of the human spirit.

ANCESTRAL SPIRITS

April Violet Shaya Ebersole

ISBN: 0-9778525-2-0

$14.95

In 1838 Mary Ann Penn's mother sang and rejoiced at the birth of her daughter, not knowing the prejudices, hardships, and injury Mary Ann was destined to endure. At a young age Mary Ann lost her mother, her home, and her Native-American people, traditions, and culture. But she ultimately triumphed over adversity, and generations later her spirit slipped into the dreams of her great-great-great granddaughter to relate a fascinating family saga. That descendant, Violet April Ebersole, developed a profound bond with Mary Ann. Feeling compelled to research her maternal ancestry and write the story of her family, April discovered that the historical record and DNA testing supported the information she had been receiving in her dreams. In 2005 April applied for recognition as a member of Mary Ann's Indian tribe.

Peppertree Press ✖

THE QUIET PEOPLE OF INDIA

Norvall Mitchell

David Mitchell, Editor

ISBN: 978-1-934246-43-6

$14.95

This book presents a unique record of the last seventeen years of the British Raj as seen through the eyes of a young officer of the Indian Political Service. Taken from Norvall Mitchell's own original memoir, written in the 1070's, his son, David, has edited the work to produce an account of a man for whom improving the lot of the masses, those "quiet people of India," met with ever-increasing frustration by the "dead hand" of British Indian bureaucracy.

FLORENCE, LOVE, ART, ARTISTS, FRAGMENTS OF MY LIFE

Giuliana

ISBN: 978-1-934246-34-4

$14.95

In Greenwich during wintertime when my internal speedometer slowed down I wrote these recollections. It was an exercise with a foreign language and a desire to emerge from the gloomy season. I had no idea then that I would publish it one day. In Florence, my native city, I met David who was studying art in the traditional classical style with two great teachers: Pietro Annigoni and Nerina Simi. David painted many views of Florence, the city that meant so much to him. Our love story was part of that scenic background of green cypresses among low red tiled roofs, and below, the Arno River reflected God's nature and the Florentine's work.

Memoirs

1605 Remodeled, Parenting at its Best

S.P. Luke Crawford

ISBN: 978-1-934246-33-7

$14.95

Parenting is a hot topic in current publishing. Raising children whether in 1930 or 2007, with changes in life style, communications, education, values, the task is much the same. Children need attention, love, respect, discipline, fun and security. The witness of my parents gave me the stamina to face challenges, disappointments, pain in life, to be unafraid of risk-taking and to enjoy success, and the panacea of laughter. My two older brothers and sisters, exhibiting a similar love of life, also march across these pages. Enjoy reading 1605 Remodeled, Parenting at its Best!

An Orphan's Song

Jean Becker

ISBN: 0-9778525-0-4

$16.95

Little Jean's life shatters on Pearl Harbor Day, when her mother, just 35, dies of pneumonia. Seven-year-old Jean and her three sisters are thrust into an unknown orphanage life, when her father says, "I'll be back soon." So much for promises. Struggling through hardships, the resilient orphans look for sunshine in a world of darkness. Worries of separation and fears about the future cloud Jean's childhood. But she never loses hope, wishing for things other children take for granted. Eventually her wishes are fulfilled.

THE DISPLACED PERSON

George Picart
Cover Art: Gregory Jacob

978-1-934246-62-7
$14.95

This is a story about George Picart's courageous family who have lost their homeland and material wealth, but not their faith, hope, and love for one another. Picart's hope is that this book will inspire other displaced families in search of freedom and their quest to be dedicated and loyal American citizens.

LIFE IN THE SANDBOX

Lenny Rifkin

ISBN: 978-1-934246-30-6
$19.95

A heartwarming and comical saga of one man's unbelievable journey.

THE TRANSPARENT VEIL, THE JUDY MITCHELL STORY

Judy Mitchell Vergason
Jan Eberle

ISBN: 978-1-934246-75-7
$14.95

The Transparent Veil is the true story of Judy Mitchell who, at the young age of 17, joined the Convent and devoted 26 years to "wearing the veil". Judy's awe-inspiring life as a Catholic sister is peppered with amazing detail, including her 11-year dedication of extraordinary mission work as a teacher in Finland. Judy's sacred existence as a nun was shaken when she fell in love with the one man who turned her world upside down. Her courageous decision to leave the Convent will pull at your heartstrings as she relives the humiliation of leaving the Convent and the disappointment she felt from those who shamed her. With the love of her husband and his commitment to serving his country with loyalty, she joined his crusade and dedication to The American Legion. Judy's Mitchell's life continues now with her undying love of God...her unforgettable memories of one man...her never-ending commitment to country.

UP ISLAND WOMAN

Hope Bailiff
ISBN: 978-1-934246-40-5
$12.95

Hope Frances Flanders Danielson Tower Bailiff was born on Martha's Vineyard in the fishing village Indians called Menemsha Creek on June 29, 1918. It was a good place and a good time to be born. She wrote this book as a collection of her memories from various stages of her life. What emerges from this anthology is the portrait of a talented and spirited woman -- in other words, she is an "Up Island Woman."

A STORY OF TWO UNCOMMON LIVES

Bernard Stein

ISBN: 978-1-934246-67-2

$14.95

The author tells the story of his life from childhood in New York City through World War II. He leads us through his years as a dentist in a New York prison with tales of many interesting patients. Intertwined is the story of his love Ilona, a holocaust victim who he met and fell in love with in postwar Berlin. They married there and were together for over 60 years.

AN ELECTRIFYING JOURNEY

William L. Mraz

ISBN: 978-0-9817572-5-4

$14.95

An Electrifying Journey is a compilation of many stories and activities that became the life of the author. As a youth he became fascinated with electricity and magnetism in its many forms and the wonders of nature first experienced in the Northwood's of Wisconsin. His education and work allowed the expansion of that fascination with contributions to engineering and a further appreciation of science and nature. These pages record the author's experiences of childhood, the Depression, WWII, a career, and retirement.

Memoirs

A Lifetime of Memories

Elsie Evans

ISBN: 0-9778525-7-1

$9.95

Written as a personal memoir to her family, Elsie Evan's "A Lifetime Of Memories" informs readers of an exciting life filled with laughter and some tears along the way. Elsie's account of events of her life will make you laugh and cry.

There's a Plunger in my Tree

Alan Handwerger

ISBN: 978-0-9817572-2-3

$14.95

If there were a list of American writers who, like Scott Fitzgerald and Ernest Hemingway, had come to their callings fully formed, and who were able from tender ages to produce great works of literature, I would not be it. I knew a quarter of a century ago that I was cut out to be a writer; yet I failed to pursue writing as my career. Instead I became a pretty decent teacher, a half-decent chef, an indifferent retailer and a God-awful industrialist. I guess I was gathering raw material. It's taken me fifty-seven years to get down to this writing business in any meaningful fashion. If I were Fitzgerald I'd have been dead thirteen years ago. Hemingway; I'd have a date with a shotgun in four years. All things considered, I'd rather be me.

30

Peppertree Press ✺

ELMER'S TUNE

Eugene Elmer Browning
and Melba Archer Browning

ISBN: 978-0-9817572-1-6
$14.95

Out of his unquestionable loyalty and love of his country, along with his faithfulness and love that he held, for the women in his life; comes this story of a young boy. He became a man after serving as a ball turret gunner in the 8th Air Force; 32 missions over Germany during WWII. He was decorated with the Distinguished Flying Cross. His love of Country came from within, from his heart and his mind, for a special universe all its very own.

THE HAND OF THE MOST HIGH

Susan Blount

ISBN: 978-1-934246-11-5

$9.95

Filled with emotional scripture and verse, Susan Blount will take you on an inspirational journey spoken from the heart and faith.

BEAUTY SCATTERED

Maggie Elizabeth McLeod

ISBN: 978-0-9814894-1-4

$7.95

This little book was written by a free spirited little girl who was so wise beyond her years. She learned many life lessons on her short stay on this earth. Please enjoy her works and find some of the secrets she discovered in being a typical teenager who loved life more than life itself.

ALL SAID AND DONE

Jack Veeger

ISBN: 978-1-934246-14-6

$14.95

Collected from 10 years of work, "All Said and Done" is poetry at it's finest. What you will find here are poems that reach to depths of visualization and thought provoking emotion. A timeless collection that can be enjoyed over and over.

HEALING ART JERSEY-STYLE,
OBSERVATIONS FROM THE LAND OF BADA-BING BADA BOOM
Robert Bedea

ISBN: 978-1-934246-45-0

$9.95

This book is about proactive poetry on the art and science of holistic health. Subjects from nutrition to spirituality are tackled in poetic fashion. It is a great blueprint for life.

AS IT IS WRITTEN
Gulf Coast Writers Group

ISBN: 978-1934246-17-7

$14.95

A collection of works from the Gulf Coast Writers of Anna Maria Island, Florida. It spans 32 members writing in all areas of specialties including poetry, science fiction, essays, and more. So, sit back, relax, and enjoy selections written by a very talented group of individuals who have joined together to showcase their skills.

HANDS-ON MINISTRY
Pastor Albert G. Yusko

ISBN: 978-1-934246-16-0

$11.95

This book is not for the "faint hearted." You will be convicted, challenged, and encouraged. In the end, you will have nuggets of truth deposited in your life.

Poetry and Inspirational

Eddies and Vortices

In a More Dimensioned World

Joe Cyr

ISBN: 978-1-934246-01-6
$9.95

This book of poems is a multifaceted exposition of human experience. The first section describes the beauty of Nature, the beauty of Woman, the beauty of Love and the beauty of the French countryside which the author visited in 2001. Next are poems intended to inspire, followed by a section on Nostalgia which describes observations from the author's childhood, and includes a delightful ride on a carousel of yesteryear.

Lauren's Story

An Inspirational Cancer Journey

Lauren Frank and Jennifer Frank

ISBN: 978-1-934246-48-1
$17.95

Lauren's Story is a joint effort between Lauren and her mother, Jennifer. Together they put together a scrapbook that shows the journey that Lauren has taken through her cancer treatment and recovery. A portion of the proceeds of the sale of Lauren's Story will be donated to organization's that support childhood cancer.

CHRYSALIS

The Venice Public Library Poets' Workshop

ISBN:

$12.95

Attending Venice Public Library poets' workshop founded in 2004 by New York poet, Jill Bart, four individuals would each from her or his notebook of poems written and collected over a lifetime. They found sharing their poems an experience to appreciate. Now after the death of their leader, Jill Bart, they would express gratitude for her encouragement and commemorate her memory with a small, late blooming anthology, titled Chrysalis.

THE PLACE

James O. Kelly

ISBN: 978-1934246-12-2

$9.95

This collection of poems will tug at your emotions and bring back memories from years past. Filled with rich visions and meaning "the Place" is poetry you will want to visit over and over again.

Children's

I'm Adopted, I'm Special

Beth Rice

Illustrator: Sharon Podgurski

ISBN:978-0-9817572-0-9

$12.95

Beth Ann is five years old and she is adopted. But what does being adopted really mean? Join Beth Ann as her colorful dream leads her to a better understanding of what adoption means in one simple message.

The Ballad of Victor the Cat

Gaile Harpan

Illustrator: Sneha Reddy

978-0-9814894-4-5

$12.95

Find out what happens to Victor, the Cat, when his fate is changed by a good man named Paul. Watch for future ballads and stories of Victor's friends; Omar, Calvin and Snowball!

The Ballad of Calvin the Cat

Gaile Harpan

Illustrator: Sneha Reddy

ISBN: 978-0-9817572-6-1

$12.95

Find out what happens when a young girl reachs out to rescue a feral cat named Calvin! How does a simple act of kindness change the lives of many? Also, you might enjoy The Ballad of Victor the Cat by the same author and illustrator. Adorable!!

EMILY "I THINK I SAW HEAVEN"

James M. Holbrook

Illustrator: Jennifer Brittingham

ISBN: 978-1-934246-56-6

$14.95

Sweet Emily was curious about heaven so, she asked her family members their thoughts. They each had a special answer for her question and she realized that everyone's ideas and beliefs were different. Enjoy the adorable illustrations and take a walk through this book with Emily.

THE PEPPER TREE,
HOW THE SEEDS WERE PLANTED!

Julie Ann Howell

Illustrator: Tiffany LaGrange

ISBN: 978-1-934246-51-1

$12.95

Grandpa always said they went together like Peas and Carrots, but Polly and Penny didn't think so. This family story is about getting along, working together and friendship. Join Polly and Penny and the scarecrow in the garden and find out what lessons they learned on that summer day.

THE SNAKE WITH A BELLYACHE

Jean Schwartz

Illustrator: Todd Fisher

ISBN: 978-1-934246-41-2

$10.95

Why does Scooter's belly hurt? After eating his meal Scooter's owner finds himself with a snake that has a bellyache! Can Dr. Stull, the veterinarian save the day...and Scooter? Find out in this delightful story.

Children's

Two Happy Stories For Kids

Joe Cyr

Illustrator: Ramon E. Owen

ISBN: 978-1-934246-73-3

$12.95

The theme of this book is Happiness! It includes subtle morals, yes, and happiness assuredly. While the stories were written for beginning readers, they are delightfully suitable for reading aloud to younger children, who will want to see the pictures, of course. Adults, too, I bet, will enjoy these two new stories by Great Grandpa Joe.

The Truth About Dragons and Dinosaurs

Edward C. Miranda

Illustrator: Andrea Cassetta

ISBN: 978-1-934246-22-1

$10.95

A Young boy learns the truth about natural history from his wise grandfather. Along the way he also learns some important truths about life...and death.

Talking to the Moon

Verner Bootsma

Illustrator: Tiffany LaGrange

ISBN: 978-1-934246-70-2

$12.95

Talking to the Moon is an adorable story about a little boy that has a wish to talk to the moon and share all of his secrets. Discover the wonders of his dream and special friendship with the moon.

Peppertree Press ✖

NIGHT TRAVELER

Dr. Karen Hutchins Pirnot

ISBN: 978-1-934246-97-9
$12.95

In this little book you just might dream of furry things, take a ride in the sky on a comet or perhaps see a rainbow dance. Anything is possible when you dream away and make the dreams come true.

KEEPER OF THE LULLABIES
A BOOK FOR GRANDMOTHERS WHO CHERISH THE WORLD OF CHILDREN

Dr. Karen Hutchins Pirnot

ISBN: 978-1-934246-90-0
$12.95

The Keeper of the Lullabies is always with the song. Imbedded in the part of love which moves the child along. The Keeper of the Lullabies is a book for grandmothers who cherish the world of children. Beautifully written and illustrated by the author, Dr. Karen Hutchins Pirnot.

I AM OF SCRAM

Gerhardt, Barbara, P

ISBN: 978-1-934246-15-3
$12.95

Meet an unhappy king whose name is I AM, who lives in a strange little kingdom called Scram. There's only one road to the kingdom of Scram, guarded by an odd-looking creature named Fram. What can change things? What can be done? Come read this story and have lots of fun.

Children's

JUNIOR & BO'S TRIP TO THE OLYMPICS

Panayotis

Illustrator: Andrew Theophilopoulos

ISBN: 978-1-934246-26-9

$10.95

In this book you will find the character Junior is going to Athens, Greece with his father and brother Andrew for the summer Olympics. This time Junior will not be able to bring his beloved dog Bo, with him on the trip, or will he?

MAGICAL TREES AND CRAYONS:
GREAT STORIES BY GREAT GRANDPA JOE

Joe Cyr

Illustrator: Ramon Owen

ISBN: 0-9778525-6-3

$9.95

The Little Crayon that Wasn't the Brightest in the Box - Olive is a crayon who wishes for the day when some one will take her out of the box and color with her. Unused by the children, Olive is very unhappy. Then, one day Olive's wishes come true when a artist shows the children the true inner beauty of Olive. The Adventures of Two Magical Trees - When a kind and lovable Canadian blue spruce named Jacques seeks adventure in Paris he meets Denise. She is a magical evergreen from Paris who loves to dance. Together Jacques and Denise share a fun adventure and become friends in this charming, and lighthearted story.

Peppertree Press ✻

A Cat's Tale,
One Cat's Search for The Meaning of Life

Lindy Lindemann

ISBN: 978-1-934246-03-0

$12.95

This book will lead you down a path to follow your dreams. So, you will find true wisdom, your special place in the world, your purpose in life and your true identity. Tom, the cat finds these things for himself during this story. This book shows that when a student is ready the teacher will appear.

The Magic Apple Tree

Jack Kendall

Illustrator: Sally Bostrom

ISBN: 0-9787740-4-3

$9.95

The Templeton family has a special tree on their farm. It grows larger, sweeter, nicer apples...it also talks. Meet the Templetons and their very special friend in this heartwarming story about a boy, his family, and the special secret they all share.

My ABC Pink Book

Written and Illustrated by: Tiffany LaGrange

ISBN: 978-0-9814894-3-8

$12.95

C is for cupcake, J is for Jelly Beans and L is for Ladybugs. This alphabet book is made special for your little sweetheart. Using fun, colorful images, My ABC Pink Book is ideal for toddlers and preschoolers. Its appealing illustrations are perfect for helping young readers learn words, letters and sounds. A great addition to any child or teacher's library.

Children's

I'm A Pefectly Normal Kid Who Happens to Have Diabetes!

Cathy Morris

ISBN: 978-1-934246-85-6

$12.95

This book is about my grandson Jack, who happens to have Juvenile Diabetes. In this beautifully illustrated book, I take you along his path of learning about this disease from hospital visits, to what to eat in order to keep his body healthy.

The Stuff In The Back Of The Desk

LeeAnn Brink

Illustrator: Aaron Cratty

ISBN: 978-1-934246-05-4

$10.95

Poor Justin! He just is having no luck at all! All the while, stuff in Justin's desk seems to be growing at a most alarming rate! Find out what happens in this funny...yet somehow scary story about a boy and the teacher that uncovers the secrets of... The Stuff In The Back Of The Desk.

The Enchanted Tree

Donna Heller and James Payne

Illustrator: David Zamboni

ISBN: 978-1-934246-72-6

$14.95

Flossie Flamingo and her friends discover a magical tree, a rainbow, and learn the importance of both healthy eating and exercise. You will enjoy reading this fully illustrated book from start to finish.

THE LITTLE HOUSE ON BUCHANAN STREET

David Wood

ISBN: 978-1-934246-64-1

$12.95

This is the story about a charming little house in Spring Lake Village, Michigan. It is written by a Grandpa who wanted his grandchildren to know the true meaning of Christmas. Between the pages each child will learn the history of the holidays as they color and read about this endearing house on Buchanan Street.

THE WORLD IS A BEAUTIFUL PLACE

A. Don Augsburger

Illustrator: Lara Ressler-Horst

ISBN: 978-1-934246-44-3

$14.95

This book is to be read to or with children to encourage awareness and stimulate dsicussion, preparing them to face the possibilities of disaster or to give assistance to children dealing with pain and suffering resulting from some form of disaster. A portion of the proceeds from sales of this book will be donated to agencies related to disaster relief.

KICKLIGHTER SHADOW & THE BEEPLES

Lindy Lindemann

Illustrator: Charles Vincent Antonsen

ISBN: 978-1-934246-29-0

$12.95

Join Kicklighter Shadow for a sweet, heartfelt story about an extraordinary elf and his adorable family, the Beeples. An adventure of discovery that not only tells a story but also teaches about friendship and happiness.

Children's

THE DUCKLING'S FIRST ADVENTURE

Shelly Perry
Illuatrator: Bonnie Loebel

ISBN: 0978774035
$9.95

A playfully suspenseful true life account of three baby ducks on their first outing. Travel with them as they meet their neighbors on the lake. See how they handle strangers and the disappearance of Mama. A delightful story for children of all ages to be enjoyed again and again.

MR. BOTHERS

Lesley Frost
Illustrator: Andrea Cassetta

ISBN: 978-1-934246-59-7
$12.95

Welcome to the world of Cydna Blodwyn Roberts. Cynda is an extremely bright and imaginative eight year old girl with a very big problem! When Cydna is bullied at school she isn't quite sure what to do. Enter Mr. Bothers, a friend that teaches Cydna how to be brave and to believe in herself. A fun, delightful story that will keep you turning pages till the very end.

Peppertree Press �

AC Heroes, Storm Surge Book One

Ron Knight

Illustrator: Dan Pedro

ISBN: 978-1-934246-86-3

$9.95

The children of the 3rd grade aftercare at Lamarque Elementary, seem to be normal to other teachers, friends, and even their parents, but everyday between 3:00 and 6:00... They are AC HEROES!

AC Heroes, Storm Surge Book Two

Ron Knight

Illustrator: Dan Pedro

ISBN: 978-1-934246-78-8

$9.95

AC Heroes was created by third graders in the after care program at Lamarque Elementary. Its purpose is for children to have something interesting to read, fun to color, and exciting to dream about. Children helping children.

Children's

CHILDREN TODAY AROUND THE U.S.A.

Barbara L. Bishop

ISBN: 978-1-934246-25-2

$14.95

Eighteen children from many states come together in this book with their pictures and stories. Each one has a different background, family and lifestyle. These boys and girls have a short story about who they are, where they live, their name and what they are doing in the picture. A map of the United States is included to enable young readers to locate cities and states. The three questions at the conclusion of each story will stimulate imagination, encourage discussion, and provide an opportunity for children to exchange ideas. Children Today Around the U.S.A. is a combination of artistic, social, educational, and economic lessons. Visually exciting and verbally stimulating, young readers will want to own and share this original book. Parents and teachers will watch children learn United States geography through Children Today Around the U.S.A. Look for future books by Barbara L. Bishop coming soon.

THE BLUE PENGUIN

Dr. Karen Hutchins Pirnot

Illustrator: Makenna Karen Klanot

ISBN: 978-1-934246-79-5

$14.95

The Blue Penguin teaches a great lesson to young readers that it is okay to just be YOU! This book teaches the reader to be proud of what you accomplish and the challenges you face everyday. The author, Dr. Karen Hutchins Pirnot is inspired everyday herself by her own grandchildren. One of them just happens to be the illustrator of this book, Makenna Karen Klanot. Makenna is in the fifth grade. Two of her favorite things are penguins and dance.

CIRCLE...THE MOON

Barbara M. Lockhart
Illustrator: Kimberly Grunden

ISBN:978-1-934246-96-2
$10.95

In this colorful book you will find shapes everywhere. Take time to pause...you might be surprised at what you see.

A COLORFUL DAY

Dr. Karen Hutchins Pirnot
Illustrator: Taryn Lane Klanot

ISBN978-0-9814894-9-0
$12.95

A Colorful Day is filled with vibrant illustrations, shapes and adorable animals. This book will bring a smile to everyone that reads it.

SAM'S PERFECT PLAN

Dr. Karen Hutchins
Illustrator: Julie Ross

ISBN978-0-9814894-8-3
$12.95

A world upside down! How could this be? You will soon find out by reading each and every page of this colorful book and discover how our friend Sam comes up with the perfect plan.

Children's

ANIMALS AND STUFF

Mark Shaber

Illustrator: Tiffany LaGrange

ISBN: 978-1-934246-10-8

$12.95

These rhyming stories are easy to understand, with words suitable for young eyes and ears.
Some of the stories contain a good lesson, and all but one of these stories is about animals and overcoming their adversities.

ZOO RENDEZVOUS

Jill Jana Marie

Illustrator: David Zamboni

ISBN: 978-0-9817872-9-2

$12.95

Have you ever wondered what happens when the guests leave, and the zoo gates are bolted shut for the night? Come inside and join the animals for a Zoo Rendezvous.

Peppertree Press ✖

Just Hanging Out,
A Collection of Poems for Kids

Khaya Dawn Klanot
Illustrator: Dr. Karen Hutchins Pirnot

ISBN: 978-0-9814894-5-2
$16.95

Follow the footsteps inside this adorable book of poems written for kids to enjoy. From Rainbows to bubblegum, nine year old author Khaya Dawn Klanot has taken her poetic words and turned them into a masterpiece. This book was illustrated by her grandma, Dr. Karen Hutchins Pirnot.

www.ingramcontent.com/pod-product-compliance
Lightning Source LLC
Chambersburg PA
CBHW080340290526
45791CB00009BA/2673

9 780981 868363